The Little Book of

Essential Foreign Swear Words

Emma Burgess

SUMMERSDALE

Copyright © Summersdale Publishers Ltd 2002

Reprinted 2002 (twice)
Reprinted 2003 (twice)

All rights reserved. No part of this book may be
reproduced by any means, nor transmitted, nor
translated into a machine language, without the
written permission of the publisher.

Summersdale Publishers Ltd
46 West Street
Chichester
PO19 1RP   UK

www.summersdale.com

ISBN 1 84024 239 6

Printed and bound in the EU.

Thanks to:
Nils Feldmann, Lisa Feldmann, Luis Zapardiel,
Lutz Luithlen and Melanie Parnell

Contents

Introduction.....................................4

Swear words....................................6

Swear phrases..............................16

Random rudeness from
around the world...............................114

THE LITTLE BOOK OF

Introduction

When you go on holiday abroad, it's important to be able to communicate with the natives. It's useful to know, for example, whether the policeman who is trying to bundle you into the back of a van with his truncheon up your arse is calling you a *bastard* or a *cunt*. With this book, you will not only be able to understand him, but you'll also be able to retort in a suitably charming manner.

Many wars have started due to language barriers. Do your bit for international accord and learn to speak in their tongue. Just make sure you wash your mouth out afterwards.

Very brief note:

As Ambassador of All Things Sweary, I am anxious that you cause great offence without further delay. Therefore, rather than confuse you with matters of gender (Le or La cul etc.) – *I'm not referring to your own gender: one would hope that you've managed to suss that yourself by now* – I have provided you with generic swearwords in their most basic, easy-to-use, boil-in-the-bag, chicken-in-a-basket, painting-by-numbers, plug-and-play, one-up-the-arse sort of way.

Happy swearing, or as the French say '*Va te tripoter*'!

THE LITTLE BOOK OF

"Arse"

French:
Cul

German:
Arsch

Italian:
Culo

Spanish:
Culo

THE LITTLE BOOK OF

"Arsehole"

French:
Trou de cul

German:
Arschloch

Italian:
Budiùlo

Spanish:
Gilipollas

"Balls"

French:
Couilles

German:
Eier

Italian:
Testicoli

Spanish:
Pelotas

THE LITTLE BOOK OF

"Bastard"

French:
Salaud

German:
Hurensohn

Italian:
Bastardo

Spanish:
Cabrón

THE LITTLE BOOK OF

"Bitch"

French:
Salope

German:
Schlampe

Italian:
Stronza

Spanish:
Zorra

THE LITTLE BOOK OF

"Bugger it!"

French:
Merde alors!

German:
Scheiß drauf!

Italian:
Maledicalo!

Spanish:
¡Me cago en la puta!

THE LITTLE BOOK OF

"Bullshit"

French:
Des conneries!

German:
Kacke

Italian:
Stronzata

Spanish:
Y una mierda

"Cunt"

French:
Con

German:
Fotze

Italian:
Fregna

Spanish:
Coño

THE LITTLE BOOK OF

"Dick"

French:
Bitte

German:
Schwanz

Italian:
Cazzo

Spanish:
Polla

THE LITTLE BOOK OF

"Dyke"

French:
Gouine

German:
Lesbe

Italian:
Lesblca

Spanish:
Tortillera

THE LITTLE BOOK OF

"**Faggot**"

French:
Pédé

German:
Schwuchtel

Italian:
Froclo

Spanish:
Maricón

"Fart"

French:
Pet

German:
Furz

Italian:
Loffa

Spanish:
Pedo

THE LITTLE BOOK OF

"Fuck"

French:
Baise

German:
Ficken

Italian:
Scopata

Spanish:
Joder

THE LITTLE BOOK OF

"Fuck off!"

French:
Va te faire foutre!

German:
Verpiss Dich!

Italian:
Vaffanculo!

Spanish:
¡Vete a tomar por culo!

"Fur burger"

French:
Hamburger de fourrure

German:
Fellburger

Italian:
Hamburger della pelliccia

Spanish:
Conejito

ESSENTIAL FOREIGN SWEARWORDS

"Piss"

French:
Pisse

German:
Pisse

Italian:
Piscio

Spanish:
Pis

THE LITTLE BOOK OF

"Shit"

French:
Merde

German:
Scheiße

Italian:
Merda

Spanish:
Mierda

"Tits"

French:
Nichons

German:
Titten

Italian:
Zinne

Spanish:
Tetas

THE LITTLE BOOK OF

"Wanker"

French:
Branleur

German:
Wichser

Italian:
Segaiolo

Spanish:
Gilipollas

THE LITTLE BOOK OF

"Whore"

French:
Putain

German:
Hure

Italian:
Puttana

Spanish:
Puta

"Your country is like a toilet. It doesn't need a President, it just needs someone to flush all the shit away."

French:

Votre pays est comme une toilette. Il n'a pas besoin d'un président, il a besoin de quelqu'un pour vider toute la merde.

German:

Dein Land is wie ein Klo. Ihr braucht keinen Präsidenten, sondern nür einen, der die Scheisse wegspült.

Italian:

Il vostro paese è come una toletta. Non ha bisogno di un presidente, esso necessità giuste qualcuno di irrigare tutta la merda.

Spanish:

Tu país es como un wáter. No necesita un presidente sino alguien que tire de la cadena para que se vaya la mierda.

Are you dribbling or do you have rabies?

French:
Ruisselez-vous ou avez-vous la rage?

German:
Sabberst Du oder hast Du Tollwut?

Italian:
State gocciolando o avete rabbia?

Spanish:
¿Babeas o tienes la rabia?

THE LITTLE BOOK OF

**Can you drink
the water here,
or does it
taste of piss,
like your beer?**

French:
L'eau est-elle potable, ou a-t-elle le goût de pisse, comme votre bière?

German:
Kann man das Wasser hier trinken, oder schmeckt es auch nach Pisse wie das Bier?

Itallan:
Potete bere l'acqua qui, o gusto di orina come la vostra birra fa?

Spanish:
¿Se puede beber el agua aquí o sabe a pis como vuestra cerveza?

THE LITTLE BOOK OF

" Please hide your face before I vomit. "

PLEASE HIDE YOUR FACE BEFORE I VOMIT.

French:
Veuillez cacher votre visage
avant que je vomisse.

German:
Bitte versteck dein Gesicht,
sonst muss ich kotzen.

Italian:
Nasconda prego la vostra faccia
prima che vomiti.

Spanish:
Por favor, tápate la cara si
no quieres que pote.

I think I might have stepped on something unpleasant. Yes, it's your country.

French:
Je pense que j'ai marché sur quelque chose de désagréable. Oui, c'est votre pays.

German:
Ich glaube, ich bin in etwas unangenehmes getreten. Ach ja, dein Land.

Italian:
Lo penso ho fatto un passo su qualche cosa di sgradevole. Sì, è il vostro paese.

Spanish:
Me parece que acabo de pisar algo asqueroso. Ah, sí. Es tu país.

**You have the
brain of a
cheese sandwich.**

YOU HAVE THE BRAIN OF A CHEESE SANDWICH.

French:
Vous avez le cerveau
d'un sandwich au fromage.

German:
Du hast das Hirn eines Käsebrötchens.

Italian:
Avete il cervello di un panino del formaggio.

Spanish:
Tienes el cerebro de
un emparedado del queso.

"If you were twice as clever, you would still be stupid."

French:
Si vous étiez deux fois plus intelligent,
vous seriez encore stupide.

German:
Und wenn du doppelt so schlau wärst,
wärst du immer noch doof.

Italian:
Se foste due volte intelligenti,
ancora sareste stupid.

Spanish:
Si fueras el doble de inteligente,
aún serías estúpido.

I wouldn't touch you with a shitty stick.

I WOULDN'T TOUCH YOU WITH A SHITTY STICK.

French:
Je ne vous toucherais pas avec
un bâton couvert de merde.

German:
Ich würde dich nicht mal mit 'nem
beschissenen Besenstiel berühren.

Italian:
Non li toccherei con un
bastone coperto merda.

Spanish:
No te tocaría ni con un
palo lleno de mierda.

Your country's quite nice, as far as leprosy colonies go.

French:
Pour une colonie de lèpre,
votre pays est tout à fait plaisant.

German:
Für eine Leprakolonie
ist Ihr Land ziemlich nett.

Italian:
Per una colonia di lebbra, il vostro
paese è abbastanza piacevole.

Spanish:
Como colonia leprosa,
tu país está muy bien.

**Put a toilet
on your head
and keep it there
while I shit on you.**

French:
Mettez un w.c. sur votre tête et gardez-la là tandis que je chie sur vous.

German:
Setz dir eine Toilette auf den Kopf und halt sie fest bis ich fertig geschissen habe.

Italian:
Motta una tolotta sulla vostra testa e mantengala là mentre caco su voi.

Spanish:
Ponte un retrete en la cabeza y aguántalo mientras yo me cago en tí.

" Shut up. "

French:
Ferme-la!

German:
Halts Maul.

Itallan:
Chiuda la vostra faccia.

Spanish:
¡Cállate!

Who won the war, anyway?

French:
Qui a gagné la guerre?

German:
Wer hat eigentlich den Krieg gewonnen?

Italian:
Chi ha vinto la guerra?

Spanish:
¿Quién ganó la guerra?

You smell like a monkey's arse.

YOU SMELL LIKE A MONKEY'S ARSE.

French:
Votre odeur est comme le cul d'un singe.

German:
Du riechst wie ein Affenarsch.

Italian:
Il vostro odore è come
il culo di una scimmia.

Spanish:
Hueles como el culo de un mono.

Your football team is shit.

French:
Votre équipe du football est merde.

German:
Dein Verein ist Scheisse.

Italian:
La vostra squadra di giooo
del calcio è merda.

Spanish:
Tu equipo de fútbol es una puta mierda.

Your mother suckles pigs.

French:
Votre mère allaite des porcs.

German:
Deine Mutter säugt Schweine.

Italian:
La vostra madre allatta i maiali.

Spanish:
Tu madre da de mamar a cerdos.

Your mother was a hamster, and your father smelled of elderberries.

French:
Votre mère était un hamster, et votre père
sentait des baies de sureau.

German:
Deine Mutter war ein Hamster und dein
Vater roch nach Holunderbeeren.

Italian:
La vostra madre era un cricelo ed il vostro
padre sentito l'odore di delle bacche di
sambuco.

Spanish:
Tu madre era un hámster y
tu padre olía a bayas de sauco.

"

Your penis is so small that if you fucked a mouse it wouldn't notice.

"

French:
Votre pénis est si petit que si vous baisiez
une souris elle ne réalise pas.

German:
Dein Schwanz ist so klein, dass es 'ne
Maus nicht merkt, wenn du sie fickst.

Italian:
Il vostro penis è così piccolo che se
scopaste un mouse non realizza.

Spanish:
Tu pene es tan pequeño que si te
follaras a un ratón, no lo notaría.

THE LITTLE BOOK OF

**Your country is shit.
Your food is shit.
Your beer is shit.
I could go on...**

French:

Votre pays est merde Votre nourriture est merde. Votre bière est merde. Je pourrais continuer…

German:

Euer Land ist Scheisse. Euer Essen ist Scheisse. Euer Bier ist Scheisse. So könnte ich weitermachen...

Italian:

Il vostro paese è merda. Il vostro alimento è merda. La vostra birra è merda. Potrei continuare…

Spanish:

Tu país es una mierda. Vuestra comida una mierda. Vuestra cerveza una mierda. Podría seguir...

I hate you!

French:
Je vous déteste!

German:
Ich hasse dich!

Italian:
Li odio!

Spanish:
¡Te odio!

THE LITTLE BOOK OF

Do you want a fight, big nose?

French:
Voulez-vous un combat, grand pif?

German:
Willst du Ärger, Großmaul?

Italian:
Desiderate una lotta, naso grande?

Spanish:
¿Quieres pelea, narizotas?

THE LITTLE BOOK OF

"

What did your grandparents do in the war?

"

WHAT DID YOUR GRANDPARENTS DO IN THE WAR?

French:
Vos grandparents
qu'ont-ils fait dans la guerre?

German:
Und, was haben deine Grosseltern
im Krieg gemacht?

Italian:
Che cosa i vostri grandi gonitori
hanno fatto nella guerra?

Spanish:
¿Qué hicieron tus
abuelos en la guerra?

Go and jump off a cliff.

French:
Allez sauter d'une falaise.

German:
Geh und stürz dich von einer Klippe.

Italian:
Vada e salti fuori di una scogliera.

Spanish:
Ve y tírate por un precipicio.

I would like to buy your children. How much is the boy?

I WOULD LIKE TO BUY YOUR CHILDREN.

French:
J'aime vos enfants.
Combien coûte le garçon?

German:
Ich mag deine Kinder.
Was kostet der Junge?

Italian:
Gradisco i vostri bambini.
Quanto è il ragazzo?

Spanish:
Me gustaría comprarte los hijos.
¿Cuánto vale el niño?

I would like to break something. Can I borrow your nose?

I WOULD LIKE TO BREAK SOMETHING.

French:
Je voudrais casser quelque chose.
Est-ce que je peux emprunter votre nez?

German:
Ich möchte etwas kaputtmachen.
Kann ich mir Deine Nase borgen?

Italian:
Vorrei rompere qualcosa.
Posso prendere in prestito il vostro naso?

Spanish:
Me apetece romper algo.
¿Me prestas tu nariz?

Excuse me, waiter. I ordered chips.

French:
Excusez-moi, garçon.
J'ai choisi des frites.

German:
Entschuldigung, Herr Ober,
ich habe Pommes bestellt.

Italian:
Scusilo, cameriero.
Ho ordinato le patatine fritte.

Spanish:
Perdón, camarero.
He pedido patatas fritas.

" Did you spill my litre? "

French:
Avez-vous renversé mon litre?

German:
Hast du meinen Liter verschüttet?

Italian:
Avete rovesciato il mio litro?

Spanish:
¿Me has tirado el litro?

This beach is taken.

French:
Cette plage est réservée.

German:
Dieser Strand ist reserviert.

Italian:
Questa spiaggia è riservata.

Spanish:
Esta playa es reservada.

Please stop talking loudly in that annoying language.

French:
Cessez s'il vous plaît de parler
fort dans cette langue irritante.

German:
Hör auf, so laut in dieser nervigen
Sprache zu reden.

Italian:
Smetta prego di comunicare fortemente
in quel linguaggio irritante.

Spanish:
Por favor, deja de hablar tan
alto en ese idioma tan molesto.

"

Honestly, officer, his face was like that when I met him.

"

French:
Véritablement, monsieur l'argent,
son visage était comme ça
quand je l'ai rencontré.

German:
Ehrlich Herr Polizist, sein
Gesicht war schon vorher so.

Italian:
Veramente, l'ufficiale, la sua faccia era
quella forma quando l'ho incontrato.

Spanish:
De verdad, señor agente, su cara
estaba así cuando me le encontré.

Are you inbred, by any chance?

French:
Êtes-vous inné, peut-être?

German:
Bist du zufällig ein Produkt von Inzucht?

Italian:
Loi ci cono uniti tra consanguinei, forse?

Spanish:
¿Eres así de nacimiento?

THE LITTLE BOOK OF

**I have you
down as
a bit of
pigeon-licker.**

I HAVE YOU DOWN AS A BIT OF PIGEON-LICKER.

French:
Je vous avez pris pour
un lèche de pigeons.

German:
Ich wette du bist
ein Taubenlecker.

Italian:
Li ooommettevo lecco i piccioni
nel vostro tempo di ricambio.

Spanish:
Te machaco.

You freak!

French:
Vous anormal!

German:
Du Freak!

Italian:
Voi strani!

Spanish:
¡Tú, malhecho!

Where I come from incest is not encouraged.

WHERE I COME FROM INCEST IS NOT ENCOURAGED.

French:
Là d'où je viens l'inceste
n'est pas encouragé.

German:
Wo ich herkomme ist Inzucht verboten

Italian:
Dove vengo dal incest non è consigliato a.

Spanish:
De dónde yo vengo,
el incesto no está bien visto.

"

Is that a suntan or do you have shit on your fingers?

"

French:
Est-ce que c'est un bronzage ou avez-vous
de la merde sur vos doigts?

German:
Bist du braungebrannt oder hast du
Scheisse an den Fingern?

Italian:
È quello un suntan o avete
merda sulle vostre barrette?

Spanish:
¿Eso es moreno o es que
tienes mierda en los dedos?

THE LITTLE BOOK OF

Random rudeness from around the world

Afrikaans

fok jou:	fuck you
jou poes:	you cunt
moffie:	queer
poes:	cunt
trek draad:	wank
sit jou kop in die koei se kont en wag tot die bul jou kom holnaai:	put your head inside a cow's front bottom and wait for a bull to take you up the arse

Arabic

biz:	tits
boos teezee:	kiss my arse
chraa:	shit
charra alaik:	shit on you
cus:	fuck you
sharmute:	bastard
zib:	nob
nek ni:	fuck me
mamhoon:	homosexual
kul khara!:	shut up!

THE LITTLE BOOK OF

Chinese (Cantonese)

ah si:	I need a shit
hail:	cunt
gai:	whore
sek si:	eat shit
diu:	fuck
diu lay lo mo hail:	fuck your mother's front botty

Chinese (Mandarin)

bil:	cunt
liu mang:	bastard
chao ni niang:	fuck your mother
dah bien:	shit
nu nu:	tits
jil ba:	nob
jiljil:	piss

Dutch

moederneuker:	motherfucker
smerige kankerhoer:	dirty cancer-suffering slut
zakkewasser:	testical washer
broekhoesten:	to fart
flamoes:	cunt
een wip maken:	fuck
lul:	nob
kwakkie:	sperm
reet:	arse
schoft:	bastard

Esperanto

anusulo:	arsehole
fek:	shit
fiki:	fuck
furzi:	to fart
kaki:	to shit
kako:	nob
pugo:	arse
patrinfikulo:	motherfucker
bugri:	to bugger
midzi:	to give a blow job

French

tu m'emmerdes:	you're pissing me off
va bouffer ta merde:	eat shit
va te tripoter:	go tinker with yourself
bloblos:	droopy tits
caca:	poo
pipi:	piss
il y a du monde au balcon:	enormously capacious knockers
foufoune:	hair pie
espece de salaud, je vais vous casser la gueule:	you bastard, I'll smash your face in
je voudrais donner un coup de poing à quelqu'un:	I want to punch someone

German

fick mich:	fuck me
schlampe:	slut
abspritzen:	to ejaculate
hosenscheisser:	someone who shits their pants
jemandem einen blasen:	to give a blow-job
moesensaft:	cunt juice
titten:	tits
reihern:	to vomit
stricher:	male prostitute

Greek

malakas:	wanker
pisoglentis:	someone who has fun with his arse
pisokolito:	back door sex
skata:	shit
hyessou:	bullshit

Hebrew

lech zayen para:	go fuck a cow
lakek et hatahat sheli:	lick my arse
zayin:	penis
ben zsona:	son of a bitch
inahl rabak ars ya choosharmuta:	go to hell with your fucking father

Italian

no me interesso un cazzo:	I don't give a shit
pezzo di merda:	piece of shit
scopa tua mama:	fuck your mother
bagnarsi:	to come in your pants
ciucciami il cazzo:	suck my nob
pecorina:	sheep-shagging
spagnola:	tit-wank
sverginare:	to deflower a virgin
quella ragazza ha la pipa bollente:	that girl has a hot cunt
leccaculo:	arse-licker

Japanese

baka:	stupid
bakayarou:	arsehole
chipatama:	dickhead
kusojiji:	old fart
kuso shite shinezo:	die shitting

Portuguese

eu estou gozando:	I'm having an orgasm
grelo:	clitoris
paneleiro:	queer
foda-se:	fuck it
vai-te foder:	fuck you

THE LITTLE BOOK OF

Russian

bl'ad:	oh shit; bitch
govn'uk:	bastard
malofya:	sperm
drochit':	to wank
ebat':	to fuck
kurite moju trubku:	suck my cock
pizda:	cunt
yeb vas:	fuck off
siski:	tits
ëb tvoju mat':	fuck you

Serbian

crko dabogda stoko

seljacka:	drop dead, redneck ox
govedo:	twat
jebem ti sunce:	I fuck your sunshine
jedi govno:	eat shit
kurac:	cock
picka:	cunt
jaje:	testicles
jebem ti staru u	
supak:	I fuck your mother in her arse
kurvo razvaljena:	fucking bitch
podudlaj mi ga:	suck my dick

THE LITTLE BOOK OF

Spanish

me cago en la leche:	I shit in your milk
hijo de puta:	motherfucker
metete un palo en el culo:	shove a stick up your arse
dar candela por el culo:	to take it up the arse
hacer la sopa:	to lick a front bottom
jugar a los dos bandos:	to swing both ways
posición de mira quien viene:	to do it doggy-style
los mangos bajitos:	saggy tits
tu madre tiene pene:	your mother has a nob
zorrero:	burglar who shits on the floor